BOOK REVIEW SECRETS FOR AUTHOR SUCCESS

HOW TO WIN GREAT REVIEWS TO MAKE YOUR BOOK SHINE

BARB DROZDOWICH

Copyright © 2018 by Barb Drozdowich

All Rights Reserved. This copy is intended for the original purchaser of this book only. No part of this book may be reproduced, scanned or distributed in any printed or electronic form without prior written permission from Barb Drozdowich.

❋ Created with Vellum

NOTE OF THANKS

I would like to thank you for buying one of my books!

I tend to focus on the technical tasks that authors and bloggers need to learn. As of this publishing I have 18 books in print and several more in various stages of completion. I'm always looking to be helpful - often creating books around subjects that I get a lot of questions on from authors and bloggers just like you.

At the end of this book is the link join my group of readers and get some free help with the technical subjects.

On to the book - I hope you enjoy and learn lots!

INTRODUCTION

There are only 24 hours in each day.

Being an author today means wearing many hats and trying to make the best use of those 24 hours.

Book Reviews can consume large amounts of any author's time and energy. Where to get these much-touted reviews? Who is qualified to review your book? What rules need to be followed? Where can reviews be shared? Is there one answer to these questions or are there many answers? Is there a different answer to these questions for some genres over others?

Do these questions keep you awake at night?

If your answer is yes, you aren't alone. My name is Barb Drozdowich and I've been working in the author world for almost a decade. I started as a book blogger in late 2009, posting reviews of library books to an ever-growing book blog. Although this started as a hobby to keep me intellectually occupied during my child's nap time, it quickly progressed into a full-time job of sorts. I grew my book review blog from a modest start to a daily audience of 800 visitors from all over the world. In addition, I have carried out two large surveys of bloggers—resulting in well over 700 submissions—and written about the results. I understand the world of review bloggers!

Although I've written extensively on bloggers and how they can help authors, this book will focus on reviews in general.

What types of reviews are open to authors? What is the purpose of various different types of reviews? We'll also talk about starting points and will debunk some common myths that exist around the subject of reviews.

I'd like to say this will be an action-packed book—but since I'm not writing a thriller, perhaps I should say that this book will be filled with actionable details for authors of any experience level. Most of my books are aimed at a beginner audience. That is the level where authors need the most help, I believe. With the topic of reviews, all authors seem to struggle at various points. This book will be focused at authors along the spectrum of their careers.

Without further ado, let's move on to describing what a review is.

1
WHAT ARE REVIEWS?

A book review can run the spectrum of a few words to several pages of critique.

Perhaps this is why it is so difficult to characterize and perhaps this is why many readers are so intimidated at the thought of leaving a review for a book they have read—they imagine it to be a much bigger deal than it actually is.

Or…perhaps readers are having flashbacks to high school English class and don't want to go there…

Regardless, we as authors need to not only get better at characterizing what a review is (so we can help our readers understand what we want them to do), but also recognize the need or use of various different types of reviews.

Let's start with what a review is, throw in some rules and then move on from there.

In its simplest form, a review can be "Great Book!" or "Loved this book." These words can be accompanied by some stars or other type of rating. As I said, on the other end of the spectrum, a review can be pages of critique on various aspects of the book. These brief, or extensive thoughts, can be sent to you by email, they can be posted on a private blog or website, a commercial blog or website, a social media site or a retail site.

With respect to these reviews, certain commercial platforms like Amazon have rules that reviewers have to follow regarding content and most commercial review-granting organizations have guidelines or expectations posted.

But for the most part, there are no rules. This isn't high school English class and the teacher hasn't just handed out a paper for an assignment.

However, a review can still be: "Great book!"

Perhaps this is the crux of the problem. How are we to help our readers understand what we want them to do unless we can be a bit more concrete?

Let's divide reviews into professional reviews or commercial reviews and reader reviews, as I'm sure you can agree the standards can be expected to be different.

A reader review is the chance for a reader to share their thoughts about what they thought of a book. Keep in mind, this is something that readers have always done—even before the creation of Amazon—we would chat with fellow book lovers. In my mind, there is nothing better than chatting about the latest book I've read. I know that urge to shout to the world about a really good book was one of the driving forces behind my book blog creation.

Since the advent of the internet, reader reviews, which were once an in-person activity, have also moved to online. Not only can readers leave reviews on their (or other's) blogs or websites, but readers are encouraged to leave reviews of books purchased from any of the book retail sites—and will likely get a reminder email from the retailer to do so. In addition, there are various social media sites like Goodreads which encourage readers to list and review books.

Several years ago I was at a conference and a presenter on the subject of reviews said that "reviews" which occur before a book is published are reviews for the author; "reviews" that occur after the book is published are for readers. I initially tried to push back on that thought, but the more I mulled it over, the more I realized how correct it was. As authors we generally see pre-publication reviews as critiques, but they are generally devices to help us improve—to polish our book before it is published. Once published, the book is available for purchase by readers; any one of those readers has the ability to share their thoughts.

We don't qualify who can and can't purchase our books. They are available for sale to anyone who has enough money to pay for them. In a similar vein, we can't control the reviews that are shared about our books. It is true that some people go out of their way to be unkind in their thoughts when reviewing, but in my experience the majority of reader reviews are honest and forthright. In many cases, reader reviews can be quite helpful to us as authors.

A short story before we move on from this topic. One of the first books I published was on the topic of Goodreads, a reader-centric social website. I was determined to explain to authors how to navigate this rabbit's warren of a site and take advantage of its powerful features. To help with the navigation of the site, I carefully created 250 color screenshots and other graphics to include in my book in order to help with my step-by-step instructions of "click on the blue button," etc. I tested the e-book on my 27-inch computer and it looked beautiful! One of the very first reviews I received was very critical and complained that the graphics were too small to be seen on a smart phone screen. My first thought was "why the hell are you reading this book on your phone?" Of course the graphics are small on a tiny phone screen. Trying to be helpful, I replied to the review and suggested the reviewer view the book on a larger screen, perhaps a desktop computer. I was told the only electronic device she owned was a smart phone—she did everything from her phone.

Although I didn't like this review, it was justified and I learned from it. The next edition of the Goodreads book had links to a video course and the screenshots and other graphics were gone.

I am the type of person who reads most reviews—especially at the beginning. I find I learn from them. That being said, if you are the type of personality that is easily thrown off by comments from readers, don't read them.

Let's move on to professional or commercial reviews—or perhaps we should call these "**non-reader**" reviews.

This is a big category and what fits in here can be open to interpretation. To add come clarity, let me define what I mean by "professional or commercial" reviews.

A professional or commercial review, whether it is something the author seeks out or not, is a review that is written by an experienced person generally following a stated set of guidelines.

As I mentioned, the reviewer is typically experienced, and may have an educational or experiential background in reviewing books. An example of this would be a book reviewer for a major newspaper or literary publication. The reviewer may be a person who is well versed in the genre of the book, or an expert in the field if the book is non-fiction. An example of this is a peer review in an industry publication for a non-fiction book.

Focusing on a commercial review—or a review that an author pays for—these reviews, generally speaking, are carried out by an experienced reviewer and follow a stated set of guidelines. Or in other words, if you purchase a review, you should be aware of what may or may not be said and what may or may not be shared publicly. We'll go into details in a future chapter, but authors should have access to an FAQ of sorts about what they are paying for and if the review is not favorable, they may have the option of preventing the review from being made public.

As I said at the beginning of this chapter, although a review can run the gamut of a few words to several pages of critique, when talking about a professional or commercial review, they are unlikely to be only several words and are much more likely to be at least several paragraphs in length or longer.

Now that we've come to the end of this chapter, are you any closer to understanding what a review is? Can you describe a review to your readers when you ask them to share some thoughts? Ultimately, it is part of our job as authors to ask our readers to leave a review. Before moving on to the next chapter, perhaps take a few moments and jot down a blurb asking for a review that you can put in the back matter of your next book!

2
WHY DO YOU WANT/NEED REVIEWS?

In today's internet savvy world, reviews are ubiquitous. They serve as social proof.

I'm sure you've noticed in the last few years, we are encouraged to share our thoughts about retail purchases, vacations or hotel stays, and even doctor or dentist visits. Even if you, like me, feel this level of social sharing to be a bit over the top, this is the world that we live in. Not only that, this is the world that our books are published in.

As such, we need to find success in this world—which means paying attention to not only the importance of reviews, but also how to actively request them.

If we go beyond the idea that reviews serve as social proof for other buyers, other potential readers of our books, what are other reasons for accruing them?

1. They establish credibility.
2. They are a form of publicity.
3. They help to introduce a book to a wider audience.
4. They can play a role in the buying process on retail sites.

5. They are an effective tool in book marketing—sharing quotes, links to reviews, etc.
6. They can be used for blurbs on your book cover.
7. One review begets another.
8. They help a book qualify for other promotional opportunities.
9. They help people learn about your book from people other than you.
10. People are sheep and will follow a crowd—if others rave about a book, readers will take their advice.

Let's see if I can flesh out some of the reasons listed above.

The first reason listed above is the fact that the presence of reviews gives your book a sense of credibility. These days, a book on Amazon or other online retailer without any reviews seems out of place. There is an expectation of reviews being present. This presence of reviews can be a strong stimulus in the buying process

On Amazon, any reviews are shown in ads that appear on the book's detail page. Displayed without any words, those stars give readers a summary of other reader's thoughts. If we move away from retail sites, blogger reviews can be shared with thousands of viewers of their blog—a great way of spreading buzz about a book.

As mentioned above, a review shared on an established book blog is a great way to spread buzz about a book. Perhaps introduce a book to a new audience. Book bloggers create posts that are easily searched and indexed by Google. Anyone searching Google and finding a blog post can be a potential new reader for a book.

It is very common for authors to either use excerpts from blurbs on the front or back cover of their book. Quotes can also be used in social media posts, advertisement copy, and other forms of publicity.

It is fairly well known that one review begets another. Whether readers agree or disagree with posted reviews, they often feel compelled to share their own thoughts. This is seen in terms of comments on blogs or reviews or comments on retail sites.

Many promotional sites require a minimum number of reviews—and usually this refers to Amazon reviews—in order to qualify for promotional packages. Many promotional companies don't independently vet submissions; they use Amazon reviews for that purpose. By that I mean, they generally set a minimum number of reviews with a minimum star number as the entry point.

The 10th point from above is about people being sheep. Perhaps there is a kinder way to phrase this, but I'm sure everyone who reads this book has picked up a book to prove it is really THAT bad or really THAT good. Or at least has a friend who's done it. If we go back to the introduction of this book, I commented on the fact that book "reviews" are not new things. Readers have been sharing their thoughts on a book just finished for many, many years. Readers just love to share their thoughts about a much beloved book. I'm sure you've had a fellow reader say to you: "You must read…" with great enthusiasm in their voice!

One last comment about reviews before we move on to learn about the current review etiquette:

Reviews don't necessarily equal sales

Although I strongly believe that reviews have to be present in order to sell a book there isn't a direct equivalency. In other words, one review doesn't equal one sale. More reviews don't equal more sales. Because of this, authors struggle to understand how many reviews they really need. There is a myth circulating that certain high-end book promotion sites require a minimum of 50 reviews to qualify. This isn't true.

Generally speaking authors should aim for 10 to 20 reader reviews on Amazon at a minimum. This will give a book some credibility and a variety of thoughts for potential buyers to read through. This will also provide a base of reviews to qualify for most book promotion sites. Lastly, book reviews—or what type of book reviews an author seeks out —should be part of a bigger picture plan and part of well-thought-out goals.

In future chapters we will talk about various types of reviews. We'll discuss the pros and cons and the realities and hopefully cut through the myths and provide some clarity.

Before we can talk about the various types of reviews, we need to talk about review etiquette— the current dos and don'ts of the review world.

3

REVIEW ETIQUETTE

I have written about review etiquette to one extent or another in a number of my books. I feel that a chapter on this topic belongs in this book also. Authors, in their haste to obtain those much-coveted reviews, and in their unfamiliarity with the medium, often step on virtual toes.

I get how much work is required to write and publish a book. I've published 18 as of this writing. I also get how attached we all get to our books. I am no different than many of you.

That being said, the internet world is a world without an eraser. Anything that you "say" online will be around for years to come. Even if you delete a regrettable comment, some enterprising soul may have taken a screen shot to preserve your thoughts for all eternity.

Back in the time of letter writing on paper, common advice given to someone who wanted to write a snappy or potentially unkind response was to write it, put it away in a desk drawer, and let it sit. Often tempers will cool over time and calmer heads serve as a better arbiter several days or a week later.

The same can be said for today. As a well-seasoned author recently said, "Turn off the computer, walk away, and have a glass of wine. See if you feel the same way after a good night's sleep."

The reality of an author's world today is they are expected to wear many different hats. It is no longer enough to write a good story and have others deal with everything else involved in publishing and selling a book. Whether traditionally or independently published, an author is expected to perform many roles—often while working a full-time job, being part of a family, and maintaining a fairly normal social life.

Many authors who can afford the expense hire out and have help with some of the activities. Many aren't in the same financial position and take on many roles themselves. Without the help of a team, there is no one to serve as a sounding board. No one to talk an author down off the ledge of doing something regrettable.

In years past, most books were published by a publishing house and author's behavior was by and large monitored by those firms. Periodically someone would go off the grid and have to be reined back in by cooler heads at the publishing firm, but it doesn't seem that bad behavior was as common an occurrence as it seems to be in today's world.

Anyone who has been in the author world for any amount of time has seen an example of an "author behaving badly." Be it encouraging fans to trash a competitor's book on Amazon to publicly having a meltdown while the world is watching, we've all seen examples.

Please don't be one of these folks!

Bad reviews of your book hurt. Absolutely!

However, there are two types of what I'd refer to as "bad" reviews.

1. Just plain mean
2. A critical analysis of issues (or perceived issues)

Let's talk about these two individually.

1. Just plain mean

Most of us can identify a mean review. It criticizes the author rather than the book or it is clearly a rant of an unhappy person. Regardless of where a review like this is found, it is best left alone. Don't try to correct this person's opinion. Don't try to comment in any way.

The label of "Troll" is one given to someone who takes great pleasure from making others unhappy. A troll will share something on the internet—like a book review—and wait to see the defense—the comments of support trying to prove them wrong. They then jump on the defense and a fight can ensue. They take pleasure in this. Hence the saying "Don't feed the Trolls." No good can come from a public fight.

Please don't take from this that you should never interact with reviewers. Just don't interact with unbalanced or nasty people.

2. Critical analysis

Generally speaking reader reviews are a chance for readers to share their thoughts with other readers. In some cases, the reader can use this forum to share their concerns. For example, a book that has the odd word or phrase in another language can be critiqued by a native speaker of this language, perhaps pointing out grammatical issues. I've seen reviews that complain about only receiving a small percentage of the book instead of the whole document. I've also seen reviews that correct niche details—like geographical details, etc. I can also add my own experience in here, where the reviewer objected to the size of the graphics when viewed on her smart phone. These types of reviews, although critical, can be helpful to an author. They give the author the opportunity to correct errors and re-issue a book to readers.

It is true that some readers will just find fault for the sake of finding fault—criticizing the book for imagined errors or criticizing the book to simply prove to the author it is an inferior product.

Authors can find value in these sorts of reviews if they can keep an open mind and not get their back up too much. Clearly, a review that complains about a potential file error resulting in a reader only getting part of the book is important and needs to be addressed. If a review points out detail errors, the errors can be investigated and changed as necessary.

Authors seem to strive for all positive reviews. This is an unrealistic expectation and, honestly, they should strive for a range in thoughts shared. Not everyone is going to love your book. What makes a good book to some, makes it horrible to others. All you need to do is read the reviews on some of history's most beloved stories to find people who didn't like them.

The key point to remember in all this talk about positive and negative reviews is that readers can tell the difference between a helpful review and a non-helpful review—a critical review and a just plain mean review.

Let's give some examples. If I were to read the reviews and there were several that commented on the book being littered with grammatical errors that should have been caught before publishing—I would give this book a wide berth. Nothing drives me battier than grammatical errors while I'm trying to enjoy a story. If a review criticized the time-period the story was set in —let's say the book was set in Regency England and the reviewer criticized that as a depressing era in England's history—I would be reaching for my wallet, as I love stories set in that era. I'm sure you can follow what I mean.

In this day of Amazon review shenanigans, have you ever looked at a book with all 5-star reviews and wondered if it is really that good? Or have those reviews been purchased?

Readers are all different and hopefully they will all have a different response to your book resulting in a variety of ratings and thoughts shared. As an artist, you want to evoke a response from your readers. I think the worst thought a reader can have is "…well…it's done now." Isn't it better for a reader to get to the end of your story and be excited to share their thoughts with someone else?

One last comment that I frequently hear: "Bad reviews ruin writing careers." Let's clarify—a whole bunch of bad reviews about crappy grammar and poor editing will drive some readers away. But "bad" reviews about a horror novel scaring the stuffing out of someone or a romance novel with "too much sex" can be a good thing.

Just like you, readers know their tastes. They know what they like and do not like. Many will pick up a book after reading reviews to see if it is "really that bad." I'm sure you can think of "really bad books" that have sold millions.

Although we will touch on this subject in future chapters, there is a lot of confusion about how to respond to reviews—either positive or negative. One of the hardest things we face as authors is to realize that someone doesn't like what we have slaved over. Authors spend untold hours writing, editing, rewriting, polishing, and so on. The ability to "turn the other cheek" so to speak is difficult for many. It is necessary, however.

Responding to a troll can get an author into trouble in a public way. You don't want to be the next "author behaving badly" to be chatted about in Facebook groups. However, many reviewers are huge fans; a comment or a word of thanks can be a huge deal to many reviewers. As I said, we'll talk about this more in future chapters, but realize that commenting back to reviewers isn't a black or white topic.

4

WHAT IS THE PURPOSE OF THE VARIOUS LEVELS OF REVIEWS?

In a previous chapter we talked about why we want/need reviews. As you found out, there are several reasons. As we'll talk about in this chapter, as authors we want to be seeking to obtain reviews from beyond the reader reviews that are seen on Amazon.

Before we address that, let's list the various types or sources of reviews and then go on to briefly talk about the purpose of each.

1. Professional/Literary review
2. Commercial review
3. Review services
4. Blogger reviews
5. Reader reviews

1) A Professional/Literary review is one that I will define as coming from a source of influence in the author community. That may be a source such as a major newspaper or magazine or it may be a literary or niche genre (industry) journal. This level or type of review fills in a number of needs. Authors frequently seek higher approval and often having their book reviewed by a major name reviewer and published in a widely read publication is a feather in one's cap. Review of a non-fiction book by an expert in the field can also be a major accomplishment. These types of reviews can be "blurbed" or quoted on the cover of the book as not only providing social proof but acclaim from an expert. These types of reviews can also serve as a way of getting a new book in front of the eyes of a large number of readers.

2) A Commercial review is one that the author or publisher pays for. As we will discuss in a future chapter, there are well-respected review institutions from which authors can purchase a review. To be clear, this is not the same as paying a reader to post a review on Amazon. There are a number of established commercial sources of reviews for fiction as well as non-fiction books. Many of these services are long standing in their history and are considered to be fair and balanced in their analysis. Many of these services are staffed with very experienced reviewers with a long history to their credit.

3) A Review Service is a group of potential sources of reviews. There are many commercial enterprises authors can pay to get their book in front of an audience of interested readers. In this instance the payment is for the contacts and the organizational services; the reviewer is not paid. In my experience, busy authors find it easier to pay a service to expose their book to reviewers—many of whom are bloggers—but can encompass a wide range of interested readers. As with other services, reviews are not guaranteed, but many of the services have a large audience with whom to share information about a book.

. . .

4) Bloggers of various stripes are well known for posting reviews of books they have read to their blog/website as well as in many cases to other niche blogs/websites. Bloggers are for the most part hobbyists. They create a blog or website to share information on their favorite subject. Whether their primary focus is reading or not, books are often reviewed on blogs of various descriptions. Although often discounted as "too much work," or viewed as small potatoes when compared to the audience of a major publication, in fact many experienced bloggers have massive audiences!

5) Reader reviews happen spontaneously as well as in response to requests of various sorts. They may be shared in a variety of ways from in person, to social sites, to retail sites. I differentiate between reader reviews and blogger reviews due to the location the review is posted. Although many bloggers are by definition readers and, like us all, voraciously buy and read books, to generalize, reader reviews are primarily found on retail or social sites.

As I mentioned at the beginning of this chapter, the savvy author will seek out a variety of reviews. As we saw above, there are reasons for different types of reviews. We talked briefly about the reasons for various types of reviews here and will expand on this information when we cover some details in future chapters.

5

WHY SHOULD I FOCUS ON MORE THAN AMAZON REVIEWS?

Much of the "expert" advice offered up to new and experienced authors alike is to focus their efforts on Amazon reviews. This advice is to direct everyone to share their review on Amazon. Some experts will advise authors to directly approach experienced Amazon reviewers—target folks who have read similar books to yours.

Although I don't disagree that a selection of reviews on Amazon are a must for authors, I disagree that focusing exclusively on Amazon is a good idea.

The primary reasoning behind this is the capricious nature of Amazon with respect to customer reviews. We will discuss in the next chapter some of the rules that reviewers need to operate under, but look in any author Facebook group, or any online forum and you'll hear tales of Amazon stripping reviews away for seemingly unknown reasons. As I've said previously, I no longer keep track of the number of reviews Amazon has taken down from my books. It's just too upsetting. I go through periods of time where I screenshot the reviews so that I have record of them for posterity—because I just know that some will disappear and I want to save the information that readers have shared.

Other than the magic disappearing act of Amazon reviews as a reason to focus on more than that one location, what are some other reasons?

- Books are purchased from more than just Amazon and readers would appreciate reading reviews prior to purchase from their retailer of choice.
- Goodreads has 75 million readers with accounts and reviews posted there are shared with account holders as well as other retail outlets.
- Authors want readers to spot reviews regardless of how they search for a book. Blogger reviews are often easily searched and found on a Google search.
- Reviews obtained from other sources—such as literary reviews or commercial reviews—can be quoted in the Editorial Review section of the book's Amazon listing.

There are more retailers of books than just Amazon and if your books are available from other places, it is nice to help with buying decisions on those locations by encouraging leaving reviews where the book is purchased. In fact, although Amazon is often the primary point of sales, not everyone purchases books from Amazon.

Many of the more minor retail sites grab some reviews from Goodreads to display to interested potential buyers.

Authors are aware that Amazon purchased Goodreads some time ago. The assumption is that reviews left on Amazon, display on Goodreads and vice versa. Not true. Although I've seen reviews disappear from Goodreads, they tend to be more stable than the ones left on Amazon.

A primary reason to focus on more than Amazon is to appeal to readers—wherever they may be found. I tend to focus on bloggers as I'm part of that community, but there are other valid reasons to see if bloggers can be encouraged to read a book. The first reason is reach. Many experienced bloggers have massive audiences. They reach beyond Amazon and many have readers from a variety of countries around the world.

The second reason to look at blogger reviews is that their reviews are searched and indexed by Google, as are Amazon listings. Although readers tend to have their favorite retailer where they search for books, it is a good idea to have a book easily found via a Google search for people looking for information there. Again, experienced bloggers tend to rank very well on Google searches.

And finally let's not discount the power and the prestige of a higher level of review. It's not only a pat on the head, it is something that can be added to the editorial review section of Amazon and other retailers, "blurbed" on a book jacket and quoted on social media posts.

As with many things in life, we need to talk about the rules that authors must be aware of. In the next chapter, we'll focus our attentions on the most important of these rules.

6

RULES

As with many things in life, there are rules associated with reviews. Quite frankly, most of us don't *actually* read the rules that we agree to abide by. Although I tend to be detail oriented, I am also quick to click on the "I Agree" button without actually reading what I'm agreeing to.

And…I could point you in the direction of rules for various sites, but I suspect many of you would be hesitant to wade through pages of formally worded stuff. Because of that, I'll include some links, but I'm actually going to cover some of the key, and often misunderstood rules that authors need to be aware of.

The platform that seems to be the most draconian at enforcing the rules is Amazon, so let's start there.

To start with, Amazon requires reviewers to have spent $50 on Amazon using a credit or debit card in the previous 12 months in order to be allowed to leave a review. This rule is a relatively recent rule and it is one of the ways Amazon is trying to cut down on people having multiple accounts to leave multiple reviews. I hear a lot of complaints about this rule. It interferes with advanced reader teams or bloggers potentially being able to leave a review. There is truth in this.

Although I want to point out that it is fairly easy to spend $50/year on Amazon, I realize that not all readers will have that money to spend and this can provide a barrier. I'd also like to point out that although as authors we focus heavily on Amazon reviews, they are ultimately **customer** reviews and should be open only to folks who have purchased the product.

The reviews must be relevant and respectful. In other words, the review must be about the story, not the speed of the shipping service or mailing envelope the book arrived in. With regards to the respectful aspect of a review, to a large degree, common sense applies. A review can't contain threatening, racist or inflammatory language. It can't contain sexually offensive language. It can't put people in danger by containing personal contact points like phone numbers or a house address.

A sticky point for many authors is regarding the appearance of conflict of interest. It is against Amazon's rules to post a review of a close friend, business associate, or family member's book. It is also against the rules to post a review of a competitor's book. I refer to this as a sticky point for a number of reasons. First, the go-to source of reviews for a brand-new author is often family and friends. Those are sometimes the easiest review requests to be made! And many authors read the same genre they write—so leaving a review on a book they have enjoyed is often what could be considered to be a competitor's book.

This whole area of rules is filled with myths, gossip, and misinformation. The common advice given to authors is to disconnect one's Amazon account from all other social media. And to only share links to their books with information stripped away so they can't be traced.

Non-techy authors assume that Amazon has the powers of God sometimes. It is easy for Amazon to determine that a review posted by a person who shares the same Amazon account or same house as the author is likely suspect. Making the assumption that Amazon is keeping track of all my 17,000+ Twitter followers and untold numbers of people who have interacted with me on Facebook is laughable especially when you consider how many authors publish on Amazon. They have better things to do with their time and their computer systems. Likewise, the assumption that the link to a book will contain special information is easily debunked with a short discussion with someone who understands how computer databases work.

Before we move on, I will admit to having untold numbers of reviews taken down from my books published on Amazon over the years. It is frustrating! Many removals are puzzling; however, I am proof that arguing with Amazon only results in problems. I've been stripped of the ability to leave reviews on Amazon for being argumentative. There are a number of larger Indie author groups that can intercede with Amazon on an author's behalf. If you find it necessary to complain to Amazon, do so through one of the indie groups, as the outcome tends to be more favorable. Find suggestions for these groups in the Appendix.

The next sticky rule from Amazon is that reviews can't be posted in exchange for compensation of any kind. It is not uncommon for authors to offer incentive for reviews to be left—entry into a draw for a gift card or other similar prize. It is also not uncommon for authors to pay for a service to arrange for reviews to be completed. In future chapters we'll talk about NetGalley and other review services which potentially interfere with this rule.

"Review exchanges" also infringe on this rule. Authors or author groups commonly arrange reviews of each other's books. It is considered to be an easy way to increase the numbers of reviews of one's book (as well as less intimidating than contacting readers/bloggers). However, if author A reviews author B's book and author B reviews author A's book, it is easy for Amazon to determine there is likely a review swap. Both reviews can be removed.

If a review is rejected for some reason, another review for the same book can't be re-submitted. Multiple reviews can't come from the same household. So, for example, if three people read the same book in a house, only one review can be left.

Authors can send readers free books, but they can't *require* that a review be left. Generally speaking, that book is considered to be a "promotional item." Reviews for "promotional items" need to be identified as such with a statement of disclaimer included in the review along the lines of "I was provided a free copy of this book for an unbiased review."

Authors can't require or incentivise readers—even members of an advanced reader team—to leave a review. It is perfectly understandable that authors want a return for their investment. Where authors get into trouble is when they put this requirement in writing and it is submitted to Amazon by a disgruntled reader.

Let's move on to other places readers can leave reviews.

I'm fond of Goodreads—a social site for readers. Although, as mentioned previously, Goodreads has been purchased by Amazon, reviews posted on one are not shared on the other and vice versa. There are two main reasons for encouraging readers to share their reviews on Goodreads:

1. 75 million readers
2. Reviews are shared elsewhere

Yes, Goodreads has around 75 million account holders according to recent numbers, and the vast majority of the account holders are readers who are interconnected with friends. This is a social site and information about who has read which book is liberally spread around the Goodreads neighborhood in a variety of ways. Secondly, reviews left on Goodreads are shared on a number of other retailers. Current examples include Google Books, WorldCat as well as many more. These reviews may help readers with buying decisions in other locations.

Although Goodreads has rules similar to Amazon's, there are many authors who have a negative view of Goodreads. I have a primarily positive view of Goodreads and see it as a reader heaven. I feel that authors can get into trouble when they don't leave their author hat at the door. Just as I mentioned in the chapter on etiquette, responding to nasty reviews on Goodreads is really not a good idea. Reviews that are in contravention of the rules (content, profanity, release of personal information, etc.) can be reported to Goodreads and left in their hands. Also, just like on Amazon, arguing about a review is not a productive use of an author's time.

In addition to Amazon and Goodreads, readers and purchasers of books can leave reviews on a wide variety of retail sites. Kobo, iTunes, and Barnes & Noble top the list of book retailers who allow for thoughts to be left. If a book is available from other than Amazon, reviews should be encouraged on these sites as well. Perhaps because there doesn't seem to be the same importance on these secondary retailers, there is not the same level of problems reported. Most of these sites will require the potential reviewer to create an account in order to leave a review. There is a minimum character count requirement in a few examples, but not the extensive list of rules that exists on Amazon.

We'll leave our discussion of rules and move on to our first type of review—that of a Literary or what many call a Formal review.

7

LITERARY REVIEWS - FORMAL REVIEWS

I previously defined a Literary review as coming from a source of influence in the author community. Many new authors see having their book reviewed by the *New York Times* as the ultimate point of prestige. Regardless of the target, in this chapter we'll talk about some ideas for an author to obtain what to them is a feather in their cap. Since the content of this book should apply to authors, regardless of what country they live in, my examples will be general rather than specific. It is my hope that the more general guidelines will lead authors to specific examples that are applicable to their country/genre/niche.

Although many authors seem to focus in on larger newspapers as a target of a literary review, not enough attention is given to other valid choices. In this chapter, I'll present a wide variety of choices—or perhaps a wide variety of directions to look in—to obtain a review. And the point that we'll come back to is a literary review comes from a source of influence in a particular community.

I'm going to divide choices for a literary review into 4 sections:

1. Primary Newspapers/magazines – i.e. *New York Times*
2. Secondary Newspapers/magazines – i.e. local paper – "local author publishes a book"
3. Author group periodicals – either reviews or features or book launch announcements
4. Industry gatekeepers

As I mentioned at the beginning of this chapter, many authors feel that a review of their book by the *New York Times* is the ultimate in achievement, but as a new author, particularly an independent author, is a review by the *New York Times* realistic?

No.

Probably not, but let's discuss. And as we discuss each type of literary review, we'll cover the audience, realistic expectations as well as what is gotten by each.

In the first group from above, what would be defined as a primary newspaper or magazine would depend on a number of factors. I'm sure many would agree that the *New York Times* seems to be a target of many, but depending on what country you live in, there may be a better choice. Perhaps the leading newspaper or news magazine of the country the author lives in is a better choice.

These choices tend to review very few books—especially when compared to the number of books published every day—and tend to choose books either from a well-known author or from a traditional publishing house. The literary world is filled with people who believe that traditional publishers are the appropriate gatekeepers of great literature.

Although I don't feel a new author is likely to get a book reviewed by any primary newspapers or magazines, I don't want to discourage those who are really set on this type of review. In terms of audience, larger newspapers or magazines can have massive audiences. Your book can be seen and read about by hundreds of thousands if not millions of readers. It can be considered to be a huge feather in the cap and the review can be quoted and referred to for years!

Most primary newspapers and magazines will have information on submissions—and yes, even the *New York Times* has submission information. Many such reviewers will prefer a galley or an advance reader copy, as they want a chance to read and review before the publication date. In other words, this requires some advance planning.

If a review from a primary newspaper or magazine is on a to-do list, take a few minutes at this point and make a list of targets of your queries.

Let's move on to what I would call a secondary newspaper or magazine. By this, I generally refer to a local (large or small) city newspaper or a magazine with a more modest distribution or a magazine that has a more local focus as opposed to an international or national focus.

Whether or not secondary newspapers review books seems to be a function of the size of their staff. Looking locally, the *Vancouver Sun* seems to still review a small selection of books, but my local city paper does not. (Vancouver, British Columbia is the largest city in the region of Canada where I live) Most smaller local city newspapers are happy to feature a local author—perhaps cover a book launch event. Even without the presence of a review, the book and the author will receive significant attention.

Coverage of a book in a publication like the *Vancouver Sun*—or whatever your local equivalent is—will bring a lot of eyes to your book. Perhaps not as many as a primary source, but still quite a few. Let's talk about realistic expectations of getting a book reviewed as a new unknown author—probably still unlikely. If the book covers a topical subject—again an example from where I live would be oil pipelines or the salmon fishing industry—there might be a higher chance of being chosen for a review. However, as I mentioned in the previous paragraph, just coverage of a "local author event" is a great start if focusing on a secondary source.

I've mentioned the audience and the realistic expectations, but don't diminish just a mention in a secondary newspaper or magazine. Authors can use the "As featured in XX newspaper/magazine" blurb truthfully!

Like the previous section, most secondary newspapers and magazines, if they review books, will have a submission page on their website (or in the publication) with instructions. And also like the previous section, most secondary newspapers and magazines would prefer to review galleys or advance reader copies. If targeting a secondary newspaper or magazine is on a to-do list, take some time and create a list.

The third on the above list is an author group periodical. Most larger author organizations produce a magazine or release of some sort. In many cases this periodical has a fairly substantial distribution. I'm going to split hairs a bit at this point and not include genre specific author organizations in this group but in the next group.

Although it isn't usually possible to have a book reviewed in an author publication, a feature in one is good publicity nonetheless. The other thing that many larger author groups offer are contests. Being able to be a contest winner is a good thing to state on a book blurb or book cover.

In terms of realistic expectations, it is generally quite easy to be featured in an author's group magazine or periodical, especially if the author is a member of the group. It is often a member benefit open to all members. This type of feature can put a book in front of a substantial audience and again, you can use the "As featured in XX magazine" in blurbs and quotes.

The last grouping is what I listed as "Industry Gatekeepers." Depending on what the genre of the book is, there are a variety of gatekeepers who can provide a review.

Let's start with non-fiction. Non-fiction books with content that focuses on a specific discipline can be reviewed by an influencer in that discipline. For example, a book written about cyber-hacking can be reviewed by an influencer in the cyber hacking industry. Many industries have their own periodicals or magazines which can contain book reviews by various influencers.

The equivalent in the fiction world can be a periodical published and distributed by one of the genre specific author organizations such as Romance Writers of America or Sisters in Crime.

Many of these organizations—either non-fiction based or fiction based—can have huge audiences that speak to interested readers. Whether a book is featured or reviewed, the audience can be very substantial, can be referenced or blurbed about. This is very realistic in terms of achieving a review or a feature. In fact, many authors I work with seek reviews from their peer authors. It's great to have a positive comment from a well-known author in your genre.

Lastly, although we are talking about reviews in this book, don't ignore the ability to have a book entered into a genre- or niche-specific award. RITA awards for romance authors are well recognized!

I hope this chapter has given you some ideas of where to look for that literary review—that nod from an influencer in your field. Literary reviews may be a lot of work, but many authors choose to put effort in that direction. If you are one who chooses to put work in this direction, I wish you luck!

In the next chapter, I'll move on to what I call Commercial reviews.

8

COMMERCIAL REVIEWS

I define a Commercial review as one that the author or publisher pays for. For authors who have been in the industry for a while, there is generally the adage that authors should never pay for reviews.

Should reviews be paid for or not?
The short answer is yes but only sometimes!

Confusing, I realize. The reviews we will talk about in this chapter are paid for but are from a well-vetted source. In other words, authors don't want to pay just anyone to review a book—they need to consider the source. It should be noted that generally speaking, an author isn't paying for a positive review; however, the author usually has the choice to have the review publicized or not.

There are quite a few commercial enterprises that offer a review service. We'll talk about a handful in this chapter. We can't cover all the services, but it is my intent to give authors enough information to find and vet other services properly.

Authors pay for a commercial review for a number of reasons. The first reason is to have an experienced reviewer share their thoughts about a book. Many authors feel this type of review offers some sort of proof that they have created a good story. Several of the commercial review services have been around a lot of years and are recognized by readers as well as industry professionals. Please don't fool yourself into thinking that a glowing commercial review—or any review—will suddenly result in thousands of sales of your book. A review—of any category—is one piece of the puzzle.

Commercial reviewers don't share the review generated on Amazon or other retail sites (although it can be quoted as an editorial review on Amazon), but they are shared in other ways. The audience of the various commercial review sites or publications are often what authors use to justify the cost of the review.

In the following paragraphs we'll cover 5 of the most common and well-known commercial review sites and their features and benefits. I'm going to divide these services into two types:

1. Trade Reviews (the examples below are: Kirkus Reviews & Foreward Reviews/Clarion Reviews)
2. Non-Trade Reviews (the examples below are: IndieReader, Self-Publishing Reviews & Chanticleer Reviews)

Kirkus Reviews (http://kirkusreviews.com)

Kirkus Reviews has existed on the review landscape since 1933 according to their website. They claim to be an "industry-trusted source for honest and accessible reviews." Their reviewers include "librarians, business executives, journalists from national publications, creative executives as well as other professional reviewers."

While they do not guarantee a positive review, they feel that an unfavorable review can be taken as valuable feedback for improvement and does not have to be publicized. The basic price tag at the time of this printing is $425US and a review can be of either a print copy or pdf of a book. The turnaround time is stated to be 7 to 9 weeks and the author receives a 250-word review.

Although Kirkus Reviews has been around the industry for a long time and is generally well respected, what makes the $425 price tag a bit easier to swallow is the publicity that comes with choosing to publicize a positive review. According to their posted stats, Kirkus Reviews' website receives 2 million visitors each month, their newsletter has 55 thousand subscribers and their *Kirkus Reviews* magazine has a circulation of 15 thousand. Not all reviews are included in the magazine, but they claim to include about 80 each month.

Foreward Reviews/Clarion Reviews (http://forewardreviews.com)

Foreward Reviews is a commercial review service that is typically put in the same category as Kirkus Reviews. According to information on their website, they have been reviewing books for 15 years. They offer two types of reviews: Foreward Reviews, which is meant for a book not yet published, and Clarion Reviews, which is aimed at books that have already been published. Both of these types of reviews are aimed squarely at Indie authors, and don't primarily cater to the traditionally published crowd. Both products offer a 450 word review including a star rating which is published in its magazine or on the website respectively. Foreward Reviews considerations must be received a minimum of 4 months prior to publication—which of course requires some advance planning. One hundred and fifty books are chosen to be reviewed for each quarterly magazine issue.

A Clarion Review is $499US as of this writing and will result in a review which critiques all aspects of a book within a 4 to 6 week delivery window. The review will be posted to their website as well as licensed to book wholesalers. From the website:

> "We're the industry's first and most trusted fee-for-review service for indie and self-publishers. We use a team of more than one hundred qualified reviewers to help you connect your stories with the hearts and minds of booksellers, librarians, and readers excited to find undiscovered indie literature."

IndieReader (http://indiereader.com)

IndieReader has existed in the Indie author space since 2009. They claim to be half the price of their competition and their team of reviews includes "working journalists, editors, librarians and published writers."

They offer a standard review for $250US which gets the author a 350 to 400-word review in 7 to 9 weeks. They include 4 and 5-star reviews in their monthly "Best Of" roundup post on *Huffington Post* as well as posted on their website. The reviews are also shared with the Association of Independent Authors (AIA) and are visible on the Ingram Book Company buy pages.

Self-Publishing Review (http://selfpublishingreview.com)

Self-Publishing review has existed in the Indie Author space since 2008. They have been featured on *Publisher's Weekly*, *The Guardian*, the *New York Times*, *Forbes*, *HuffPost* and *Writer's Digest*. They have partnered with BookBaby and are a member of the National Book Critics Circle.

The price for their reviews range from $139US to $329US (as of this writing) with the lower priced product receiving a 200 word review without stars and not much in the way of advertising to the upper end receiving a 500+ word review with a star rating and various different promotional activities. SPR claims to have 188,000 website visitors monthly and 5300+ subscribers to their newsletter.

Chanticleer Book Reviews
(http://www.chantireviews.com/)

Chanticleer Book Reviews is a commercial review service that offers a number of interesting features. It was established in 2010 "to give all authors an equal chance at success." Their review team is comprised of "experienced editors as well as other authors, journalists, booksellers, librarians, professors and avid readers from across North America." They are affiliated with Alliance of Independent Authors, IBPA, and writers associations, including AWP, PNWA, WWP, UCWA, Sisters in Crime, Historical Writers of America, and more

Let's talk about their reviews first. They offer a commercial review for $395US with a turn-around of 6 – 9 weeks. This review will range from 350 to 800 words (depending on the genre). The author will also receive leader quotes, which can be used for stand-alone marketing and book blurbs and a star rating. The review is published to their website, e-zine, and e-newsletter (subscribers stated in the thousands) as well as their social media platform. If a review is not positive, the author has the choice to not have it publicized.

In addition to their website and various publications, they also are quite active at regional bookseller trade shows and books they review can be displayed to booksellers. Chanticleer is physically located in the Pacific North West.

. . .

Now that we have finished the chapter on Commercial review, take a few moments and perhaps a pen and paper to collect your thoughts on what you've learned. In the next chapter, we'll move on to Review Services.

9

REVIEW SERVICES

Although not a type of review, but more of a source of reviews, review services are handy to be aware of. Many authors are just too busy, or don't have the contacts to get a large number of reviews—especially when a book is first launched.

These services, for a fee, will offer a copy of a book up for reading and reviewing to an audience and in many cases will also help with the technical aspect of getting the copy of a book onto a Kindle or other electronic reading device.

I'll mention one service in this chapter, but please find links to other services in the Appendix of this book.

NetGalley has been around for quite a few years—appearing on the bookish scene shortly after I started book blogging. NetGalley is a commercial service which, for a fee, offers digital galleys (ARCs) or digital copies of published books to professional readers and reviewers and helps promote new and upcoming titles. From their website:

> "Professional readers – reviewers, media, journalists, bloggers, librarians, booksellers and educators – can join and use NetGalley at no cost."

Readers and reviewers can set up an account for free and request to read whatever books look interesting. Publishers or authors pay a fee to offer a book (or a collection of books) to account holders. They have the ability to pick and choose whom they want to read and review by looking at each requester's profile and approving only those they feel fit their audience.

As of this writing, although accounts for reader/reviewers are free, authors/publishers pay a fee. The fee for one title is $699.00US for a year or $450.00 for a 6-month period. There are discounts available from partner organizations as well as other services.

Although NetGalley doesn't publish the number of account holders, it is considered to be significant—especially with respect to media representatives and librarians. NetGalley has different versions of its service available for reviewers in Australia, Canada, France, Germany, Japan, the US and the UK.

Many blog tour or promotions companies offer a reviewing service as part of their service offerings. Many of these companies have mailing lists of thousands of bloggers and will help spread the word about a book available for review (for a fee). Please see the appendix for a list of some of the companies providing this service.

As we approach the end of this chapter, keep in mind that if you choose to pay for a company to help obtain reviews, the practice is looked on with skepticism by Amazon. The fee that is paid to companies such as NetGalley is not forwarded to the reviewers—it is a fee that covers sharing of information about a book as well as the logistics of storing copies of a book and downloading that book to reviewers. Nonetheless, this is a sticky area. Reviewers who review a book from one of these services are often advised to put a disclaimer in their review—something along the lines of "I received a book from NetGalley for my unbiased opinion."

When considering hiring a service to help obtains reviews for a book, consider several factors.

1. Audience – How many contacts does the service have and how likely are you to get some reviews? Many services will

give a guaranteed minimum number of review and others will offer the number of reviewers they have connections with. **Note** – just because a service has connections with a large number of reviewers doesn't mean you will receive a large number of reviews. Remember genre matters!
2. What does this type of review get you? – Most services offer reviews, but not necessarily reviews posted to Amazon. Reviewers that have connections to these sorts of services will share their reviews in a variety of ways. NetGalley encourages reviewers to share their thoughts on their platform. Bloggers will often post on their blog. Many reviewers will post on Goodreads, but rather than assuming, ask where the reviews will be posted.
3. Realistic expectations – As with any service, some are better than others. Make sure that what you want will be achieved by the service you choose.

Moving on from the topic of review services, in the next chapter we will start learning about bloggers and their role in the review landscape.

10

BLOGGERS

Who Are They?

I've done several surveys of bloggers and have heard back from over 700 of them. I can say with certainty that bloggers are primarily hobbyists—in the case of book bloggers—reading and reviewing books for free, for the love of books. Are there some bad apples in the bunch? Yes. As with any collection of people, there is a spectrum. In my experience, most bloggers are fair and balanced and love sharing their thoughts to their audience.

To quote from my book blogger book:

> *"...they can be male or female, they can vary in age, be quite computer literate, or just barely holding their own as far as technology is concerned. They may be teenagers, sharing their love of Young Adult (YA) as they conquer their high school classes; they may be stay-at-home moms spending their free time sharing their thoughts on their favorite books as an escape from the kids; they*

may be budding authors using a book blog as a way to experiment with their writing. A book blogger may be a parent/child duo, with the parent encouraging the child to read more. They may be newly retired, looking for a mental challenge and a way to share their lifelong love of books."

What type of bloggers?

Bloggers are identified by the material they share on their blogs and websites. If their primary focus is books, they are referred to as book bloggers. If the primary focus of a blog is travel, we refer to that person as a travel blogger. If the primary focus of a blog is lifestyle subjects, we refer to that person as a lifestyle blogger. I'm sure you can follow where I'm going with this.

Regardless of the primary focus of a blog, many bloggers read and share their thoughts on applicable books on their blogs. An important point to remember is that the audience of a blog tends to share interests with the blogger. Along this vein, a lifestyle blogger may be interested in your vegan cookbook and have an audience that would be interested in reading a review and buying a copy of the book.

Authors are told to focus on book bloggers, but I disagree. They should not limit themselves to book bloggers to get reviews for their books. Wherever there is an appropriate audience, there is a potential reviewer.

What can bloggers do for you?

Another common question I get from authors is "What can bloggers do?" The source of the question is two-fold—either the author just doesn't have a clue about bloggers and the question starts the inquiry from ground zero in terms of knowledge—or they know a little about bloggers and are curious about what range of promotions bloggers can carry out.

Starting from ground zero, bloggers are generally hobbyists. Although this is a fact I've mentioned previously, it bears repeating. Most bloggers start blogging out of a love of their primary topic—wanting to share this interest with a larger audience—not with the intention of making money. And generally speaking, bloggers who have been blogging for a long time develop an extensive audience. If this audience is interested in the topic of a book, they likely will be interested to read about it and perhaps buy a copy.

Book Bloggers are usually set up to provide a variety of types of promotions for authors. They commonly review books, but they also often participate in blog tours, release day promotions and other types of feature posts. Some bloggers can offer reviews as well as a variety of promotional opportunities. Each blogger will make their own rules and likely posts a review policy/promotional opportunities page to help authors understand what they do and don't do.

Authors tend to focus on obtaining reviews, and reviews are the focus of this book; however, as I'm fond of pointing out, to read a book and create a thoughtful review is generally 6 or 8 hours of work. A promotional post can be put together in about 15 minutes. The information is shared with the same audience. Many authors in my experience don't think about the time required for a review. They just want some attention for their book and think the only way to get that attention is by asking for a review.

When approaching a busy, experienced book blogger be sure to ask for whatever feature they have time for! In the next chapter we're going to move on to the subject of how to find bloggers - a question I commonly field.

11

HOW TO FIND BLOGGERS

In my experience, authors who are just starting out, and in particular, new authors who are not very technical, struggle to understand what bloggers are, let alone how to find some. They may ask a few fellow authors, they may ask Google some questions, and the lucky ones will actually stumble on one of the already existing databases of bloggers.

Let's flesh this out.

Asking fellow authors if they know any bloggers can be a valid starting point—as long as the authors you ask write the same genre as you do. Remember, just like you have favorite genres to read, so do bloggers. If all your writer friends write significantly different genres than you, move on to the next suggestion of how to find bloggers.

My next suggestion is a Google search. I have had authors make fun of my suggestion of doing a Google search as this can easily get an author in the weeds with hundreds of thousands of search results to wade through. This can be true. However, a Google search can also help you better target your search for bloggers.

I'll explain.

Google searches websites and blogs the world over. Doing a basic Google search is something that authors are likely quite familiar with. It has become a fairly normal activity in today's world. Search results are presented in pages ranked from the most popular (or the most likely to match what you are looking for) to the least. Generally speaking, Google will return hundreds of thousands if not millions of results to any search, but we usually only go through the first 5 or at most 10 pages of results.

Searching Google for "blogger" or "book blogger" is too generalized a search and won't return any helpful search results. Searching for "book blogger romance" might be a better search if you were looking for bloggers who are interested in romance novels. However, there are better choices that will give you better results.

Take a few moments and make a list of authors and book titles that are similar to yours. I know many authors feel their book is quite unique and no other book is really the same. That may be true, but generally speaking, a book fits into a selection of roughly similar books.

Once you have a list of books and authors, go back to Google and do some more targeted searches. Search for "Book title by Author name review." If I use myself as an example, I would search for "How To Write Non-Fiction by Joanna Penn review" or "How to Write Non-fiction review." Remember the search results will be ordered in importance so likely the first couple of pages of results will be Amazon listings or Goodreads listings. Look beyond that and you will find reviews posted by bloggers.

Why go to this trouble?

What you will find if you play with this sort of searching on Google are bloggers whose posts rank fairly well on Google (and therefore will be easily found), who have read similar books to yours, and if they liked your competitor's books, they will likely enjoy yours.

Investigate these bloggers and see if they are taking submissions. Look at how they are talking about your competitor's books, and if fair and balanced, add them to a list of bloggers to investigate.

Moving on from the idea of doing a Google search to the next point on my list—already existing databases of bloggers. Like many things on the Internet, websites come and go (often fairly quickly), but there are several databases that have been around for a number of years and are fairly well kept up to date.

http://www.theindieview.com/indie-reviewers/
http://bookbloggerlist.com

The above 2 sites are current as of this writing. **The Indie View** has been around about 5 or 6 years and seems to still respond to queries. **The Book Blogger List** is my site and has been in existence for just over 4 years at the time of this writing and has listed over 4,000 bloggers. My site is organized by genre of interest and The Indie View is an alphabetical list, and both sites are searchable. Both sites are free and open to authors searching through the listings, but neither acts as the "middle-man" sending on queries to the bloggers. You will need to click on links and visit the blogs that you are interested in.

The first step that I suggest is to create a list of bloggers you are interested in. Visit their blogs and comment—make some friends. Don't just pepper every blogger who looks remotely interesting with a query or review request.

How to find quality bloggers?

When looking for reviews from book bloggers, I suggest focusing on the review being posted on a blog. Some book bloggers will post on Amazon and other retailers, but I primarily focus on the blog. Because of this, the audience of the blog is important. Although it's lovely to have anyone share their thoughts about a book, when it comes to reviews an author seeks out, they should try to find bloggers with significant and appropriate audiences.

Let's deal with the easy part of this first—an appropriate audience. Generally speaking the reading tastes of an audience matches the content of the blog to one extent or another. An author trying to get a review for their book should seek out bloggers who demonstrate an interest in the genre they write. Seems obvious, doesn't it? I know from years of experience that beginner authors will seek out any blogger regardless of taste in reading. I'm not sure if this is due to an unfamiliarity with the blogger world or just not giving enough big picture thought to what the author wants to accomplish.

Regardless of the source, it is not uncommon for me to be asked to read a book completely outside of my stated tastes.

The audience is a difficult concept for many beginner authors to wrap their heads around. Although authors may be approached for a review copy of their book by a blogger, many of the blogger reviews will be ones that the author seeks out deliberately. To help understand how to evaluate a blog, I've created a video (https://www.youtube.com/watch?v=ZRzpqDuyBcU&t=6s)

As we come to the end of this chapter, I encourage you to take a few moments to write down some thoughts from all the information we covered. List some bloggers, jot down some thoughts about how you are going to search for bloggers, etc. In the next chapter we will move to the topic of how to query a blogger successfully.

12

HOW TO QUERY

In this section we are going to talk about "The Query." The short description of a "query" is a note to bloggers to ask for a review of an author's book (or other type of feature). Most publishing houses and agents require a query letter when submitting a book for their consideration. If you have approached agents or publishing houses, this should not be an unfamiliar task for you.

A few words about genre before we move on. When asking for a review of your book, you want to ensure that your book is in "friendly" hands. Why badger a blogger into reading your horror novel when they state they only read romance? Their one-star review will likely complain about the content of the book. Someone like me, who doesn't like having the stuffing scared out of me, won't appreciate a book that does this. I would be more likely to complain about the content than to praise it as a horror fan would do. Likewise, when asking for some sort of promotion, the book should be promoted to an audience that's likely to buy a copy.

If we take the example from above, why try to promote a Horror novel on a Romance site? Not many of the readers of that blog would be interested in buying a copy, as they don't like scary books; they like romantic books.

As I often say: "Why go to the time and effort to promote your book in a place where you aren't likely to generate any sales?" Make sure you're likely to get the "biggest bang for your buck."

In a previous chapter we covered how to find quality bloggers to review your book. Making use of the list created when finding appropriate bloggers, we're going to create one email at a time in the form of a query.

The first step in creating a query for a blogger is to bring up the website/blog of the first blogger on the list on your computer and find the page of information or instructions that needs to be followed. This page is typically called a "Review Policy" or "For Authors" or some similar label. This information should be scanned to ensure the blogger is still taking submissions and they fit the needs of the author.

As I like to remind authors, more than 50% of all bloggers receive queries for more books than they can possibly read. Don't create a note that will end up in the trash bin. Follow the instructions, and stay away from cookie cutter form letter-ish notes.

I like to point out what NOT to do first—get those things out of the way.

Bloggers notoriously don't like getting a query that smacks of a form letter, so try to create a personalized note. Look through the blog or website to find the blogger's name—don't resort to addressing the note to "Dear Sir/Madam" or "Dear Blogger"—a friendly "Good morning" or "Hi there" would be better. Do not automatically attach a copy of your book to your query. Not only is this presumptuous, but it is also a recipe for a book to be pirated.

Most bloggers will state what they want contained in a query note, but for those who don't give specifics, the following is a good general list:

- State what you are seeking in the subject line – 'Review of XX book,' or 'Promotional feature request.'
- Hopefully address the blogger by name. If not, a general salutation as mentioned above.
- In the body of the note reiterate what you are interested in.

State the title and give some information about the storyline of the book. Share the publisher, genre, release date and length. These facts matter to many bloggers—let them make an informed decision. Provide the official blurb for the book and either provide a link to an excerpt or if published, provide the Amazon link so that the blogger can easily read the sample available on the "look inside." Attach the cover graphic and let the blogger know what formats are available for reading. Most bloggers will read an electronic version of a book, but some will prefer a paperback.

- Always a good plan to include a variety of places where the author can be found online. Many bloggers want to be part of a team—they want to see the author's history of participating as part of their promotions.
- Lastly, be clear about time issues if they exist. If you are looking for help with a new release buzz, the blogger may not be able to meet time constraints. Many experienced bloggers are booked months out.

I'm sure you are looking at this list, thinking it would be easier to just send a bunch of form letters. It would be; however, experienced bloggers have the choice of a huge number of books to read or feature. Make sure the bloggers are given a reason to choose your book. Also, give them a reason to NOT hit the delete button.

Now that you understand what a query is and what it contains, we're going to move on to talk about what can be found contained in a review.

13

WHAT DOES A REVIEW ENTAIL?

Once a book is published, beginner authors are sent out to accumulate reviews for their book. Whether their publisher or their fellow writers push them in this direction, beginner writers are often either not given much guidance or not given accurate guidance in this search for reviews.

In this section we will focus on reviews by book bloggers—which may or may not be posted to Amazon. We're going to ignore the Amazon part and we're going to focus on what is posted on the blogger's blog.

Many new authors don't give much thought to the contents of a review. They just want a review, hopefully many of them! As was mentioned in previous chapters, commercial and literary reviews often have to meet a series of guidelines and the author knows in advance what the end product will look like. Take a few moments and think about what you want the review to contain. Jot down some notes.

We'll move on to what you will likely see.

. . .

First the basics:

Most blogger reviews will contain some or all of the following:

- Title/Author/Publisher/ISBN/ASIN info
- Direct links to Amazon and other locations for purchase
- Blurb or book description
- Cover art
- A summary with or without spoilers of the story line
- An analysis of the story—the blogger's opinions
- Links to the author's website/social media
- A rating system that may be simple or very complex

In my opinion, many authors, in their rush to obtain the coveted review don't actually read the types of reviews the blogger posts. I've had authors complain that certain reviewers don't give books a rating out of 5. Many don't and state this fact in their review policy. Not to mention, likely none of the blogger's published reviews have ratings, if the author had only looked. There are places where reviewers do have to leave a number or star rating, but their own blog is run by their own rules.

I've read reviews that assign a rating to every aspect of the story. To me, that seems like too much work! I've also seen reviewers who assign a letter grade from A to F and ones that will use part numbers, for example, rating a book 4.25/5.

To each his own. But again, we're back to the question of what do you want to walk away with from a review?

As I mentioned above, many authors are just focused on obtaining reviews they don't concentrate on the content of the reviews. Here's a list of things you may or may not have thought of when it comes to reviews. Perhaps compare this to the list above.

- Is a rating system of some sort important?
- How extensive do you want the system to be? Do you want to see ratings for various aspects of the story or just one overall rating?
- Do you want the book blogger to post her review to other places than her blog (i.e., Amazon, Goodreads, etc.)?
- Do you want to target a book blogger who seems to have a large following and therefore gives you lots of publicity?
- Do you want to target a book blogger who is very active on social media and has the ability to publicize her thoughts to a large audience?
- Do you want the book blogger to supply you with some quotable quotes?

I hope these points gave you something to think about. Bloggers will often work the hardest for an author who wants to be part of a promotion team. Yes, bloggers want to read and review books, but they also want to bring some attention to their blog. Be sure to follow up on all reviews bloggers share.

14

READERS OF YOUR BOOKS

One obvious source of reviews is the average reader—the person who picks up a book on Amazon or another retailer and decides to share their thoughts when they are finished.

Reviewing might be a normal activity for some readers. Many will leave reviews without prompting. Many will not. Leaving a review is not a normal or automatic activity for them. There are ways to help all readers remember to leave reviews.

Most of the retailers prompt readers to leave reviews, especially purchasers of e-books. Amazon is probably the most persistent of all the retailers in reminding readers to share their thoughts.

When a reader gets to the end of any Kindle book a screen will appear asking the reader to give the book a star rating out of 5. This rating, if only stars, isn't shared on Amazon, but the reader is offered the opportunity to enter a headline and a review comment with a minimum of 20 words. If they fill out that information, the review is posted to Amazon under their username. (The username associated with their Kindle account) The same thing will happen for books purchased from other retailers to one extent or another.

Amazon (as well as other retailers) will also send out an email a designated period of time after a purchase asking the reader (or purchaser) to review the book (or item if not a book). Some readers, if they haven't already shared their thoughts, will follow the link on the email and leave a review.

The author can influence reviews as well by simply asking. It is not uncommon for the author to add a short call to action in the back of the book—in the back matter—which thanks the reader for choosing a book and asks for a review to be left. Some readers will pay attention and follow through with a review.

Lastly, authors can ask members of their mailing list to leave reviews for books. If the newsletter is sent out to all subscribers (as compared to a unique selection of readers often called a street team or an ARC team) the request is often a more generalized request for readers to leave reviews for books that they have read.

Try to make sure that all your bases are covered when looking for reviews.

CONCLUSION

We have reached the end of this short book. At the beginning I commented on the fact that reviews can consume large amounts of an author's time and energy. That will be true whether they understand the arena of reviews or not. I hope with all the information we have covered that you have a better understanding of the subject of reviews, have jotted down some notes as you have progressed through this book, and are ready to head out into the world of reviews with a better understanding.

Although this was touched on in various sections, I hope you keep in mind that reviews of a book are only one part of the marketing puzzle. To spend all your marketing dollars on a commercial review isn't smart, but a commercial review that is a small part of an overall plan may be a good thing. Likewise, spending valuable writing time seeking out a literary review is not a good idea unless it is part of a larger marketing plan and viewed as such. The same can be said about all of the various types or sources of reviews. Because of this, I encourage you to sit down, collect your thoughts and put together a big picture of what you want to do with your book—what your goals are and how you are going to achieve these goals.

I honestly wish you luck. I do my best to help authors understand technical details that are often a bit fuzzy to the average creative person. My contact points and books can be found on the next few pages. Drop by and say hi.

…And I'd appreciate a review of this book if you have found it helpful in your understanding of the world of reviews!

APPENDIX

Lists of Indie author groups who can intercede with Amazon

Alliance of independent authors (https://www.allianceindependentauthors.org/)
Indie Author Support Network (https://www.facebook.com/groups/authorsupportnetwork)

Lists of rules

Amazon rules
https://www.amazon.com/gp/help/customer/display.html?nodeId=202094170
https://www.amazon.com/gp/help/customer/display.html?nodeId=201929730
https://www.amazon.com/gp/community-help/customer-review-guidelines-faqs-from-authors
Barnes & Noble

https://help.barnesandnoble.com/app/answers/detail/a_id/2129/kw/review
https://help.barnesandnoble.com/app/answers/detail/a_id/784/kw/review
Kobo
https://www.kobo.com/help/en-US/article/5056/managing-books-in-your-kobo-account

Sources of Literary reviews

https://en.wikipedia.org/wiki/Category:Book_review_magazines

Sources of book reviews - promotion sites

Author Media - http://authormedia.com
Bewitching Book Tours - https://bewitchingbooktours.blogspot.com
Book and the Bear - https://www.booksandthebear.com/services-1/
Book Junkie Promotions - https://bookjunkiepromotions.com/services/
Book Savvy Public Relations - https://www.booksavvypr.com/services/
Book Unleashed - https://bookunleashed.com/author-services/
Buono Amici Press - http://buoniamicipress.com/author-services/
Chapter by Chapter - http://www.chapter-by-chapter.com/blog-tours/
Chick Lit Plus - http://chicklitplus.com/services/blog-tours/
Enchanted Book Promotions - http://www.enchantedbookpromotions.com/
Enticing Journey Book Promotion - http://www.enticingjourneybookpromotions.com/p/blog-tours_18.html
France Book Tours - https://francebooktours.com
Goddess Fish Promotions - http://www.goddessfish.com/services/virtual-book-tours/

Great Escapes Book Tours - http://www.escapewithdollycas.com/great-escapes-virtual-book-tours/
Historical Fiction Virtual Book Tours - http://hfvirtualbooktours.com/tour-packages/
iRead Book Tours - http://www.ireadbooktours.com/tour-packages.html
Italy Book Tours - http://www.italybooktours.com/our-virtual-book-tour-packages.html
Jean Book Nerd - http://www.jeanbooknerd.com/p/tour-pricing.html
Lola's Blog Tours - http://www.lolasblogtours.net/
Lone Star Literary - http://www.lonestarliterary.com/promote.html
Partners in Crime - http://www.partnersincrimetours.net/tour-options/
Promotional Book Tours - http://www.promotionalbooktours.com/book-tours/
Providence Book Promotions - http://www.providencebookpromotions.com/tour-pricing/
Pump Up Your Book - http://www.pumpupyourbook.com/
Pure Textuality PR - https://puretextualitypr.com/
RABT Book Tours - http://www.readingaddictionvbt.com/
Read Between The Lines Blog Tour Services - http://www.rbtlreviews.com/
Rock Star Book Tours - http://www.rockstarbooktours.com/
Smith Publicity - http://www.smithpublicity.com/
The Children's Book Review - https://www.thechildrensbookreview.com/dedicated-review-submissions/media-kit/kids-book-tours-online-blog-tours
WNL Virtual Book Tours - http://wnlbooktours.com/virtual-tour-packages/
Writer Marketing Services - http://writermarketing.co.uk/prpromotion/blog-tours/
Xpresso Book Tours - http://xpressobooktours.com/services/
YA Bound Book Tours - http://yaboundbooktours.blogspot.ca/

GLOSSARY

Author Interview – a series of questions that are answered via email and posted on a blog

Author Platform - also known as the on-line presence of an author – made up of a blog, website presences, newsletters and various social media accounts and is used to share information with readers and communicate with readers.

Badge – A badge is a graphic that is used to advertise a blog or a website. Typically it is small and square (250px X 250px) and reflects the branding of the website.

Bitly - Bitly is a free URL shortening service that provides statistics for the links users share online. Bitly is popularly used to condense long URLs to make them easier to share on social networks such as Twitter.

Blog – A blog is a type of website which allows information to be added in a static fashion as well as a serial fashion. It can be run on a wide variety of platforms or programs such as WordPress, Blogger, SquareSpace, etc.

Blog Feed/feed – The Blog Feed or as is it is typically shortened to just Feed is also known as RSS or RSS feed. A Blog feed or a RSS feed is a standard Internet technology that allows updates of your blog to be delivered various places – other websites like Goodreads or into feedreaders like Feedly. In terms of format, it is typically your blog's URL followed by a slash and then the word 'feed' or http://yourdomain.com/feed. It is possible that your blog's feed is different.

Blog Tour Company – a business that arranges blog tour and other promotional events for a fee.

Blog Hop – A Blog Hop is an activity – or a game – that is played using blogs with posts of a common theme. All the people joining or playing the blog hop create a post on their blog and then a clickable list is created of all the blogs that are participating with direct links to each post. This allows participants to easily click on links or hyperlinks and visit the blog posts of all the participants. Often the linking of the blogs is done using a free service called Linky (there are also paid versions of this type of service) Linky will provide a form for entering each blogs' details and will create code that can be placed on blogs allowing the list to be displayed on all blogs and automatically updated as other join.

Blogging Platform – A Blogging Platform is the program that is used to operate or run a blog. There are several – the most popular among the list are WordPress, Blogger and Tumblr

Blog reader/feed reader – A blog reader or feed reader is a program that will gather the RSS feeds from blogs and display them to be read. Typically this program provides a pleasing reading format and a method of keeping track of what has been read as well as what hasn't.

Book Blogger – a book blogger is a person who has a blog who's main focus is books.

Book Blog Tour – an event involving a book/author visiting a selection of blogs during a defined period of time (same as Virtual Book Tour)

Book Blurb Feature or Spotlight Feature – a display of cover graphic, blurb, buy links, author information & links and perhaps an excerpt on one or more blogs

Boosted Posts – Without paid advertising, only 0.02% of posts are seen. This means that Facebook content from brands is often 'boosted' to increase its visibility. This involves a budget, which sends the content to a selected audience based on demographical and behavioral data.

Branding – Branding is the combination of the look, feel, and tone that creates a unified and identifiable collection of information

Cover Reveal – a posting on a blog or a series of blogs showing the cover graphics of a new book or an upcoming release – may be accompanied by a blurb and perhaps pre-order links

Domain – also known as a URL – it is the address of a website. It is typically in the format of http://yourdomainname.com

DRM encryption – DRM stands for Digital Rights Management. It is the type of encryption that is added to ebooks to control the use, modification and distribution of copyrighted material. It is used for more than ebooks as it can be used for software as well as music.

Footer – The footer is the space at the very bottom of your website or blog. In some cases is can hold information in addition to a copyright statement.

Giveaway – an item or group of items that are given away to the winner(s) of a contest

Go Viral – this is a colloquial term to indicate massive dispersal. When talking about a blog post or a Facebook post, if it is referred to as Going Viral, it attracts a lot of attention in the form of hits, shares, likes or whatever is appropriate for the particular platform.

Gravatar – a Gravatar is a graphic that represents something – often a person. As an example, a gravatar is often seen beside any comment that a person makes on a blog post or in fact a Facebook or Twitter post.

Guest Post – a blog post posted on a blog that does not belong to the author

Header – the Header is the part of a website at the top of the site. It generally runs from side to side across the top of the site. Can also be used to refer to the top of a post – the area where the title is seen.

Hits - How many people have visited your web page or blog. Monitoring the quantity of hits you receive could indicate how well your material is resonating with viewers or customers.

Hosting company – A Host or Hosting company is a business that has a collection of servers or big computers and sell space on those servers for people to run a blog or website. Examples would be Site Ground, GoDaddy or InMotion

Hotlink – Hotlink is a common term to refer to a link that is attached to an image or some text in a website or blog. If a person clicks on that picture or text they are taken to another website. As an example if a cover graphic of a book is 'hotlinked' to an Amazon buy link or URL, when it is clicked on the direct buy page for that book on Amazon is opened.

Impressions - An impression refers to a way in which marketers and advertisers keep track of every time ad is "fetched" and counted. Can also be used to refer to social media posts.

Influencer – A social media user who can reach a relevant audience (whether large or small) and create awareness about a trend, topic, company, or product. They have established credibility with their audiences, and marketers work to build relationships with them in order to reach those audiences.

Keyword(s) – A Keyword is an important word or collection of words that are used to describe something. Keywords for a book would be words like the genre, the city the book is centered in, the time period the book is set it. Keywords for an author often refer to works they use to describe themselves, their work and content for their platform communications.

Linky List – Linky or Linky List is the common term that refers to a software program or a website that allows for the gathering of information of like-themed blog posts and the display of these links on all the blogs involved.

Meme – a Meme is a game or group activity that is played on blogs and/or social media. There is a common theme, a loose collection of rules and an identifying feature. For example there is a blog meme called Follow Friday that bloggers can play. They create a blog post, post the unifying graphic and often comment on the weekly theme. They add their URL and other details into a Linky List and then go visiting other participants. Likewise a Twitter meme called #MondayBlogs has bloggers post a tweet with an eye-catching title, a direct URL and the hashtag MondayBlogs to their Twitter stream. They then retweet and visit and read the tweets/posts of other participants.

Menu bar – a Menu Bar is typically a line of clickable links either just under the header of a website/blog or in the header area of a website. The clickable links lead to other parts of the website or blog.

On-line publicity – ongoing promotional activities which can encompass book blog tours, guest posts, as well as additional marketing strategies

Organic Reach - Organic reach refers to the number of unique accounts that have see your content on social media without the use of paid promotion tools.

Paid Reach - Paid reach refers to the number of unique accounts that have viewed your content with the addition of paid promotion.

Plugin – a Plugin is a piece of code that is added to a blog that is used to perform a function on that blog. An example of a Plugin is Akismet – it helps segregate spam into a specific folder. Sometimes a Plugin can also function as a Widget. If that is the case it will have a function on the sidebar of a blog or website. An example of that would be an Image Widget.

Post or blog post – A post on a blog is a collection of words and pictures that are published and then visible on that blog. The word Post is frequently used to refer to an entry (often words and pictures) put on Facebook, Twitter or other social media.

PR Representative – person or company who manages various promotional activities – can include book blog tours, but may also include in person events as well as on-line events

Reach - Reach is a word that refers to the potential size of audience. It does not mean that that entire audience will see a social media post, but rather tells you the maximum amount of people your post could potentially reach. Reach should not be confused with Impressions or Engagement.

Review – a collection of thoughts regarding (in our case) a book.

Search engine – A Search Engine is a very complicated computer program that searches a collection of websites to find entries for given words. An example is Google.

SEO – SEO stands for Search Engine Optimization. SEO is a collection of activities that we perform on blogs/websites that make it easier for search engines to find them and search them. These activities range from careful use of keywords, to linking to other blogs, to addition of helpful information to pictures among other examples.

Sidebar – The Sidebar is the area on one or both sides of a website or blog. It contains content that is placed there often in widgets or gadgets.

Social Proof - Social proof refers to a psychological phenomenon in which people seek direction from those around them to determine how they are supposed to act or think in a given situation. In social media, social proof can be identified by the number of interactions a piece of content receives or the number of followers you have. The thought is that if others are sharing something or following someone, it must be good.

Social Selling - Social selling is a sales concept in which representatives leverage the power of social communication to engage with prospects by answering their questions, providing helpful content, clarifying information, etc.

Tags – The word Tag or Tags has many meanings. Most commonly it refers to bits of HTML coding with specific meaning. The H1 tag stands for Heading 1 tag – meaning the highest level of heading. An "em" tag stands for italics and a "strong" tag stands for bold. Tags are said to be 'wrapped' around text. Tags have their own language of a sort where <h1> means start the h1 and </h1> means stop the h1. So, to wrap the text - <h1>The Title is Here</h1> will make the phrase 'The Title is Here" the main title of a blog post. Likewise Here will make the word "Here" appear bold.

URL – The URL is the direct link or hyperlink to a post. It is can referred to as a Domain, but can also be used to show the exact link to a specific entry on a website.

Virtual book tour – an event involving a book/author visiting a selection of blogs during a defined period of time (same as Book Blog Tour)

Website – a site on the Internet that displays information about a topic/person – it may or may not be updated regularly.

Widget – A Widget is a collection of code used to perform a specific function (usually) on the sidebar of a website or blog. An example of a widget is an Image Widget that is used to hold a picture on the sidebar of a WordPress blog.

YOUR HELPFUL HINTS ARE WAITING...

Interested in getting some helpful hints and some helpful videos to your inbox. As I'm sure you are aware, authors are encouraged to give away free book to encourage people to join their mailing lists.

My books are different - they solve a problem. Just because you picked up one of my books doesn't mean you want a free book on a completely different topic. Because of this, I offer subscribers to my mailing list, free help - usually in the form of blog posts or YouTube Videos. I let everyone know about new releases and offer money off of my online courses.

If this sounds like something you would be interested in, join me at: http://bakerviewconsulting.com/reader-list/

ABOUT THE AUTHOR

Social Media and Wordpress Consultant Barb Drozdowich has taught in colleges, universities and in the banking industry. More recently, she brings her 15+ years of teaching experience and a deep love of books to help authors develop the social media platform needed to succeed in today's fast evolving publishing world. She delights in taking technical subjects and making them understandable by the average person. She owns Bakerview Consulting and manages the popular blog, Sugarbeat's Books, where she talks about Romance novels.

She is the author of 18 books, over 50 YouTube videos and an online Goodreads course, all focused on helping authors and bloggers. Barb lives in the mountains of British Columbia with her family.

Barb can be found on her Book Blog, Business Blog, Pinterest, Google+, Goodreads, and Youtube

As well as:
barbdrozdowich.com
barb@bakerviewconsulting.com

ALSO BY BARB DROZDOWICH

All my books start with a problem that needs a solution - with a group of authors letting me know about a subject that they don't understand. I take it, break it down and see if I can add some clarity.

The books I've written attack the subjects of:

1) Understanding the world of Book Bloggers and Book Reviewers

2) Understanding all the parts and pieces of an author's online presence at a beginner's level

3) Understand the world of book promotions

4) Understanding What to blog, How to blog and Why to blog for authors

5) Understand how to use Goodreads as a tool of networking and communication with readers

6) Understand mailing lists and newsletters

7) Understand how to self-publish a book

During a recent workshop I gave on self-publishing, I walked participants through an exercise to help them understand the power of e-readers as well as the limits of e-readers. I was talking about the fact that not all e-readers can make use of clickable links as not all are connected to the internet or have browser capabilities. We also talked about creating links that readers from a variety of countries can actually use - my example was around solely using an Amazon.com link. Suddenly the light went in my own head about all of the clickable links I put in my books. So…going forward I'm directing everyone to a page that contains information about all of my books and buy links that are associated with those books. The link is easy to type in manually or click on if you have the ability. It is: https://readerlinks.com/mybooks/733

Below find a short description of each of my books and don't hesitate to use the link above to find out more information in terms of formats available and places to purchase a copy.

The Authors Guide to Working with Book Bloggers

This book is the first book I wrote and is centered around information I received in a survey of book bloggers. This information has been updated through a second, more extensive survey. It is meant to serve as a primer for authors just entering the world of book bloggers or book reviewers. It helps explain the world of reviewers so that authors can walk confidently into that world and get some attention for a book.

More information: https://readerlinks.com/mybooks/733

The Author's On-Line Presence: How to find readers

This book attacks the subject of "what is an author's on-line presence?" Whether we use the word 'presence' or 'platform,' many beginner authors are intimidated by all the information swirling about the internet. The list of "must do" seems totally overwhelming. This book breaks down this subject into easy to understand chucks in normal language.

More information: https://readerlinks.com/mybooks/733

The Author's Guide to Book Promotions

This book was also borne out of many discussions with authors. What is a book blog tour? What is a promotional newsletter? How do I determine which promotion company to use? I break down the language and explain this world in easy to understand English. This book also has large lists of book tour companies as well as book promotion companies which will help you start your search.

More information: https://readerlinks.com/mybooks/733

An Author's Guide to Goodreads: How to Network with Millions of Readers

Goodreads seems to the site with so much power yet creates so much frustration in authors. I often describe this site as a rabbit's warren because of how difficult it is to navigate. This book will walk you through all aspects of how to effectively use Goodreads to communicate with readers. It also has a **Free course**

More information: https://readerlinks.com/mybooks/733

Top Advice for Authors Promoting Their Book and Book Blogger Survey

As I've mentioned previously, I've carried out several surveys of bloggers and written about the results. My first book, The Author's Guide to Working with Book Bloggers is the first book based on survey results. The two books pictured above are also based on survey results. The first one is simply the unfiltered collection of answers to the question: "If you could give an author one piece of advice about promoting their book, what would it be?" This book lists all 500+ responses. The second book is a full analysis of all 30+ questions. If you are interested in finding out real information about the book blogging/book reviewer world, these books will help.

More information: https://readerlinks.com/mybooks/733

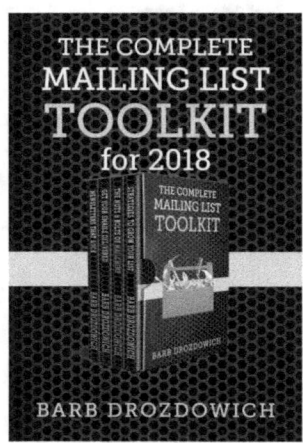

The Complete Mailing List Toolkit

I like to say that this book covers mailing lists and newsletters from soup to nuts. It doesn't focus on one aspect of communicating with readers, it covers it all. Each section is available individually and this book also has a free course associated with it.

More information: https://readerlinks.com/mybooks/733

The Author's Guide to Self-Publishing For Canadians and How to Self-Publish a Book

Both of these books are quite similar in terms of content. I really wanted to write a book focused at self-publishing for my fellow Canadians - hence the first book. The second book is similar content but without the specific Canadian content. The references are applicable for writers in any country.

More information: https://readerlinks.com/mybooks/733

www.ingramcontent.com/pod-product-compliance
Lightning Source LLC
Chambersburg PA
CBHW050040080526
44586CB00014B/1384